How to Find
AN EXTRAORDINARY DENTIST

Dr. R. Anthony Matheny, DDS, FAGD, FA

Copyright © 2018
Dr. R. Anthony Matheny, DDS, FAGD, PA

Performance Publishing Group
McKinney, TX
All Worldwide Rights Reserved.

All rights reserved. No part of this publication may be reproduced, stored in a retrieval system or transmitted, in any form or by any means, electronic, mechanical, recorded, photocopied, or otherwise, without the prior written permission of the copyright owner, except by a reviewer who may quote brief passages in a review.

ISBN 13: 978-1-946629-33-3
ISBN 10: 1-946629-33-2

Contents

Introduction 1

Traits of an Extraordinary Dentist 3

1. Reputation 5

2. Modern and clean 13

3. Answers all of your questions 15

4. Empathy 19

5. Continuing education 23

6. Latest Equipment 27

7. Great lab 31

8. Follow Up 35

Conclusion 37

Testimonials

"I had no idea that there were so many differences between dentists and dental offices! After reading this book, I definitely have a feel for what I want and don't want in an office, and I won't settle for anything less than an extraordinary dentist!"

~Bonnie Gero

"What an eye-opener! I feel I can now confidently pick an extraordinary dentist. You may have to weed through several to find one that fits the criteria, but for you and your family's health, it's worth it!"

~Kim McGinnis

"Since I live too far away to be able to go to Dr. Matheny, I'm thankful to have this book! It has saved me a lot of time in narrowing down a dentist to go to for my family. I hate to just pick someone at random, you never know what you are going to get. It is a great resource!"

~Thomas Clarich

"My husband and I are going to be doing a lot more traveling out of the area, seeing the country.
Of course, we will see Dr. Matheny when we are in town, but we may be forced to see other dentists as emergencies arise on the road. I'm glad I know what questions to ask others in order to pick a great dental office!"

~ Donna Mogler

Conclusion

Hopefully, after reading this mini-book, you can see just how one office can differ from another. It is worth doing your research before choosing an office as opposed to just randomly picking one out of the phone book. After all, this is your health that we are talking about. I believe most dentists are good and try to do well, but, unfortunately, this doesn't apply to everyone. Patients are often fearful of the pain they may experience. As you have read, there are ways to make the experience more comfortable.

I think you realize by now that not all offices and dentists are created equal. Some have chosen to see a high volume of patients, take shortcuts, charge cheaper fees than most, and create a higher stress environment for the employees and patients. I had a sign once in my office that said, "Beware of bargains in brain surgeons, parachute makers, and dentists!" Your oral health directly affects your overall health. So, spend a little time doing your research to find an extraordinary dentist! You deserve it!

Yours in better dental health,
Dr. R. Anthony Matheny,
DDS, FAGD, PA

Dr. R. Anthony Matheny

Website: **www.drtonymatheny.com**
Email: info@drtonymatheny.com
Toll-free number: (844) 366-4004
Facebook: **https://www.facebook.com/drtonymatheny**
LinkedIn: **https://www.linkedin.com/in/drmatheny/**
Instagram: **https://www.instagram.com/dr.tonymatheny/**

MAKING ONE PERSON
SMILE CAN CHANGE
THE WORLD.
MAYBE NOT THE
WHOLE WORLD,
BUT THEIR WORLD.

Introduction

Many times, patients are faced with a situation where they are in need of a dentist, but they don't have one they can call, that they know, like, and trust. They had one in the past, but had a bad experience and have not gone back to them or anyone else since. Or they have moved to a new area and have yet to find a dentist. Most people hate to just pick a dentist at random, not knowing what they are going to get.

As a consumer, it is hard to know how to find not just a *good* dentist, but an extraordinary dentist. I wrote this book to guide you through the ways to find and judge whether a dentist or an office you are considering is truly extraordinary. Here are the top ways:

> **I WAS CREATED TO CREATE BEAUTIFUL SMILES.**

Traits of an Extraordinary Dentist:

1. The doctor and office have a great reputation in town.
2. The office is modern and clean.
3. Friendly, personable staff members and doctor take the time to listen to you and answer all of your questions.
4. The doctor and staff treat patients with empathy and compassion.
5. The doctor is very competent and believes in advanced training and continuing education.

6. The office emphasizes patient comfort, utilizing the latest techniques and equipment designed to allow the patient to have very little or no pain.

7. The doctor and team don't try to be the cheapest, don't cut corners, and use great dental laboratories and quality materials.

8. The office follows up with you after bigger procedures to make sure you are feeling okay and don't need anything, and there is an emergency number to reach the doctor after hours.

1

Reputation

They have a great reputation in town.

I personally would want to go to a dental office that is well established and has a reputation for doing great dental work, makes the visit as comfortable as possible, and has wonderful customer service to take care of any need I may have. I would find out about their reputation by asking others in town and reading testimonials and reviews that other patients have left on Google, Facebook, Yelp, and other sites. If a friend, family member, or co-worker refers you to a dentist that they go to, consider asking some or all of the following questions:

YOU DON'T HAVE TO BRUSH ALL YOUR TEETH -
JUST THE ONES YOU WANT TO KEEP.

---

7 Questions to ask a family member, friend, or co-worker about their dental office:

1. How long have you been going to that dentist?
2. Have you had much treatment done there?
3. What do you like best/least about the office?
4. Does it take you long to get in when you need an appointment?
5. How gentle is the dental hygienist and dentist? Do they do anything to make the visit more comfortable than other offices?
6. Do they seem to see too many patients at once? Does the office seem hectic?
7. Do they work with insurance, and do they have payment plans available?

Once you feel comfortable calling an office that you have researched, choose from these great questions to ask when the dental receptionist answers the phone:

> **BE NICE TO YOUR DENTIST. HE HAS FILLINGS TOO.**

7 Questions to ask the receptionist when you call a potential dental office:

1. Has the doctor had any advanced training beyond dental school? If so, what?
2. How long does it take to get an appointment for a cleaning or consultation?
3. Do you have a website that I can look at or testimonials I can read?
4. Do you get your dental work done by the dentist you work for? (This is a great clue to see how good the work is. If employees won't have the doctor treat them, you shouldn't either.)
5. Do you work with my dental insurance?
6. Do you have any financing or payment plans available?
7. I am concerned about being comfortable during my dental visits. Are there any things your office does to make my experience there more comfortable?

You don't have to ask all of the questions on the above two lists. Simply choose those most important to you. These questions can give you a lot of insight into the office you are considering. Between reading the reviews and getting answers to some of these questions, you can get a good feeling as to whether you'd like to go to that office and give them a chance to see if they meet your needs.

A SMILE IS THE PRETTIEST THING YOU CAN WEAR.

BE TRUE
TO YOUR TEETH,
OR THEY WILL BE
FALSE TO YOU.

Modern and clean

I know this goes without saying, but in a healthcare office especially, you want the office to be clean. If the place was filthy, I would wonder how sterile things are and if I could get an infection in that environment. I would also not like to see equipment that is 30 years old. My feeling as a patient is that if all the equipment is 30 years old, then the dentistry techniques being performed might be that old, too. I'd be thinking that if the dentist hasn't kept up with modern technology, then maybe he/she hasn't kept up with learning the latest and greatest dental procedures. One may have nothing to do with the other, but many patients like me would jump to that conclusion.

We want every aspect of our patients' experience to be that of a modern, clean, and attractive dental home. We have computers in every room and utilize several modern technologies to make the dental work of the highest quality and greatest comfort for our patients.

3

Answers all of your questions

Friendly, personable staff members and doctors who take the time to listen to you and answer all of your questions.

There is nothing more frustrating than going to a dentist's or doctor's office, walking in, being taken to a treatment room in the back, and having the doctor or dentist walk in and have one hand on the doorknob trying to get out of the room as fast as possible while you have questions you want to ask. The second thing that aggravates me is that nobody wants to take the time to explain anything. They don't often take time to explain the problem, the benefits of the treatment, what will happen if I don't do it, the specifics of the treatment itself, how long it will take, if it will hurt, if my insurance will cover it, what to do if the insurance company won't pay, and if there is a payment plan. Because I am an analytical guy and like to have the details before I make a decision—especially a large financial one— it literally seems like pulling teeth (excuse the pun) to get all the information you want and need from many healthcare offices.

Because I like to have all the facts myself, I will give all of the facts a patient wants or needs to know. From the beginning, I've told my team that I don't care how busy I get or how many patients want to see me, I am always going to take the time to explain the problems, go over what I can do to help them, take the time to listen to them, and answer all of their questions. Not only do I insist on having time to communicate with my patients, but I want enough time to do my best work, which is dentistry at the highest level possible. It is hard for me to do top dentistry if I am rushed and there are many patients waiting on me. I treat every patient's mouth like a canvas, and I am the artist.

USE YOUR SMILE TO CHANGE THE WORLD. DON'T LET THE WORLD CHANGE YOUR SMILE.

Empathy

Doctor and staff treat patients with empathy and compassion.

Extraordinary offices treat patients like family (the family you like, that is! Ha! Ha!) This means not recommending procedures to generate income for the business only, but because it is truly what the patient needs and/or wants. Sometimes the most expensive treatment plan for the patient is not the best option for them. Usually this is the case, but not always. For example, if a patient has front teeth that are brittle and discolored, some dentists might recommend crowns on the teeth. This would be good as long as the foundation around their teeth is good, meaning there is adequate bone around the teeth and the patient doesn't have advanced gum disease. If this is the case, sometimes a denture is a better option for the patient.

Patients often come in feeling embarrassed because they have neglected their mouths for one reason or another. They feel bad that the condition of their mouth is not good, but they are having a problem that can't wait any longer. The last thing the patient needs is for the doctor or staff member to pass judgment on them or make them feel worse than they already do about the situation. Extraordinary offices understand this view, and they comfort the patient, explaining that they are there to help regardless of the condition of their mouth.

At our office, if a patient expresses that they feel bad about their mouth or that they don't want us to see how awful their mouth is, we often tell them to not worry, that we see patients ten times worse than them every day. We tell them, "No matter how long it has been, it is never too late to get healthier." We say, "We are not here to judge, just to help in any way we can." This is being empathetic and compassionate. Patients can tell by looking in your eyes and the tone of your voice whether you are recommending treatment to benefit them or yourself. So, if you get a vibe that an office is putting high pressure on you to purchase a product or service that you don't feel you need, simply go get a second opinion somewhere else. We welcome second opinions and, of course, they are at no charge.

> **MAKING THE WORLD A BETTER PLACE, ONE SMILE AT A TIME.**

Continuing Education

Very competent doctor who believes in advanced training and continuing education.

If I was picking an extraordinary dentist, I would feel better going to them if they didn't end their learning at dental school. Every dentist has to take a certain number of continuing education hours to renew their license every two years, but these hours can be taken in courses that teach older techniques or cover information that was taught many years ago.

I would be impressed to see a dentist that has completed other programs after dental school with multiple certificates or other credentials to show that he/she has been committed to continual learning and staying up on the latest and greatest techniques and procedures. As a patient, I don't really want my dentist to be doing 30-year-old dentistry on me.

I have never stopped being a student first and a doctor second. After dental school, I completed a general practice residency to learn more skills to benefit my office and patients. I went on to complete the entire program at the Dawson Center for Advanced Dental Study. Since then, I have worked towards and received my fellowship in the Academy of General Dentistry. Besides serving as past President of the Treasure Coast Dental Society, most of my years in practice, I have exceeded my minimum number of seminar hours. I always want to offer my patients the most comfortable, and latest and greatest services for their dental health.

A SMILE TAKES
BUT A MOMENT, BUT
THE MEMORIES OF IT
LAST FOREVER.

Latest Equipment

Emphasizes patient comfort utilizing the latest techniques and equipment designed to allow the visit to have very little or no pain.

One thing patients fear most when it comes to the dentist is the thought of experiencing pain. Many people have had one or more bad experiences at a dental office in the past, and no matter how many years it has been, they never forget about it.

This usually means that they won't come into the office like they should because of this fear or anxiety. The one thing that most people dread is the injection of the anesthetic, novocaine. Injections are no fun anywhere in the body, but those in the mouth are probably the most dreaded by patients. Don't be afraid to ask if an office you are considering has a process to make the injection process more comfortable.

Most dental anesthetics are a liquid solution that is acidic. Because of this, it stings and burns to some degree going in, and it takes a little time for the body to neutralize the solution and absorb it into the nerve. Some offices have a way to buffer the anesthetic, after which it is not acidic going in, thus reducing the discomfort and allowing for better and faster effect of the anesthetic.

There is also an instrument called the "Dental Vibe" which is a handheld device that has soft rubbery prongs that lies against the gum tissue and vibrates in the area where the injection will be given. This is a big distracter for the nerve and makes the giving of the anesthetic much more comfortable. Ask the office you're calling if they have the Dental Vibe or if they buffer their anesthetic.

At our office, we have both ways to make the numbing procedure much more comfortable than in the past. Most patients have stated that they have felt very little, and in many cases nothing, when I have administered their anesthetic. The Dental Vibe and buffering of the anesthetic have been a huge success.

THERE IS ALWAYS
A REASON TO SMILE.
YOU JUST HAVE TO
FIND IT.

7

Great Lab

Doesn't try to be the cheapest, doesn't cut corners, uses great dental laboratories and quality materials.

The problem is that dentistry is not a commodity, like buying a television. If you are buying a 32-inch RCA smart TV and the same TV is at Best Buy, Target, and Walmart, then you would usually buy it wherever it is the cheapest. Dentistry, on the other hand, is not the same everywhere.

There are differences in the materials used. Some cost more but are much stronger and last a lot longer. There are also differences in dental laboratories that make the crowns, bridges, and dentures. Some use cheaper materials that may not look as good or last as long.

There are also differences in the steps taken to complete the service or restoration as well as time taken to complete it. Often you get what you pay for. A friend told me once, "Nothing good is cheap, and nothing cheap is good." This is not always the case, but more times than not, it is from my experience.

We take as much time as it takes to do high quality dental treatment. We use great dental laboratories and do all dental work on our patients the same way we do it on our own families. There is a saying: "All dentists know what their dentistry is worth." The first thing I think about when someone or some company is much cheaper than others is "What are they leaving out, and what is not as good as it should be?" It makes me very suspicious. Our goal is to provide dentistry in the top 5% in the nation at a cost that is average or slightly above, so we are still providing great value!

BE THE REASON
SOMEONE
SMILES TODAY.

Follow Up

The office follows up with you after bigger procedures to make sure you are feeling okay and don't need anything, and there is an emergency number to reach the doctor after hours.

Many times, a patient will have multiple fillings, crowns, or extractions done, and then they go home. Occasionally, a patient may have a problem such as pain or swelling, or simply has a question about what they can or cannot do. The problem is that nobody has called to check on them and sometimes there is no phone number available to reach the doctor after hours. That would not be a good feeling if you were a patient in this situation.

This is why I call and check in on all patients that have had bigger procedures done to make sure they are doing okay and don't need anything or have any questions for me. I can't tell you how many patients have been surprised that I, as the doctor, actually took time to call and check on them after hours. They are very appreciative and thank me. I am happy to do it. It is the right thing to do, and it is what I would want.

www.ingramcontent.com/pod-product-compliance
Lightning Source LLC
Chambersburg PA
CBHW070040070426
42449CB00012BA/3122